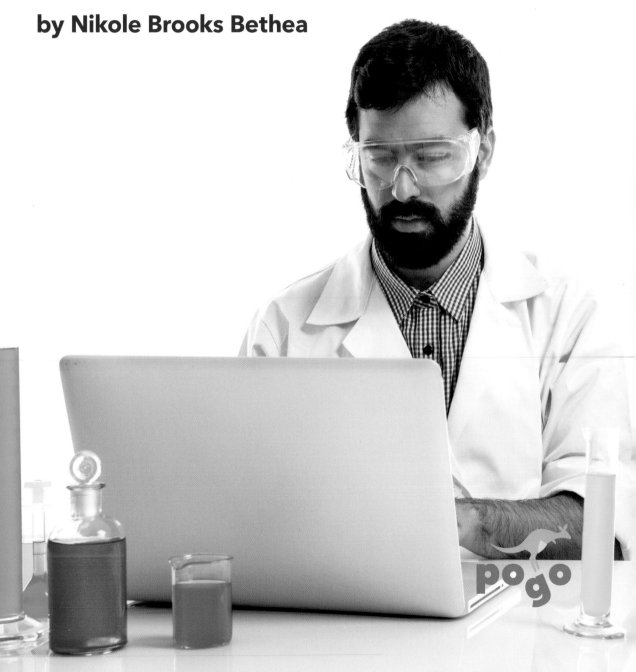

STEM CAREERS
PHYSICIST
by Nikole Brooks Bethea

pogo

Ideas for Parents and Teachers

Pogo Books let children practice reading informational text while introducing them to nonfiction features such as headings, labels, sidebars, maps, and diagrams, as well as a table of contents, glossary, and index.

Carefully leveled text with a strong photo match offers early fluent readers the support they need to succeed.

Before Reading

- "Walk" through the book and point out the various nonfiction features. Ask the student what purpose each feature serves.
- Look at the glossary together. Read and discuss the words.

Read the Book

- Have the child read the book independently.
- Invite him or her to list questions that arise from reading.

After Reading

- Discuss the child's questions. Talk about how he or she might find answers to those questions.
- Prompt the child to think more. Ask: Do you know anyone who works as a physicist? What projects has he or she been involved in? Do you have any interest in this kind of work?

Pogo Books are published by Jump!
5357 Penn Avenue South
Minneapolis, MN 55419
www.jumplibrary.com

Library of Congress Cataloging-in-Publication Data

Names: Bethea, Nikole Brooks, author.
Title: Physicist / by Nikole Brooks Bethea.
Description: Minneapolis, MN: Pogo Books, published by Jump!, Inc., [2019]
Series: STEM careers | Includes bibliographical references and index. | Audience: 7-10.
Identifiers: LCCN 2018017786 (print)
LCCN 2018025405 (ebook)
ISBN 9781641281911 (ebook)
ISBN 9781641281904 (hardcover; alk. paper)
Subjects: LCSH: Physics—Vocational guidance—Juvenile literature. | Physicists—Juvenile literature.
Classification: LCC QC29 (ebook)
LCC QC29 .B48 2019 (print) | DDC 530.023—dc23
LC record available at https://lccn.loc.gov/2018017786

Editors: Jenna Trnka and Susanne Bushman
Designer: Michelle Sonnek

Photo Credits: Dr Project/Shutterstock, cover (equations); James Hoenstine/Shutterstock, cover (calculator); Tungphoto/Shutterstock, cover (notebook); photastic/Shutterstock, cover (pencil); Luis Molinero/Shutterstock, 1; Andy Dean Photography/Shutterstock, 3 (child); Vankad/Shutterstock, 3 (equation); zhgee/Shutterstock, 4; Bernd Mellmann/Alamy, 5; ShutterStockStudio/Shutterstock, 6-7; Ranta Images/Shutterstock, 8; sspopov/Shutterstock, 9; SuperStock/Science Fiction Images/Age Fotostock, 10-11; Tyler Olson/Shutterstock, 12-13; memorisz/Shutterstock, 13; science photo/Shutterstock, 14-15; Scharfsinn/Shutterstock, 16-17; naluwan/Shutterstock, 18; wavebreakmedia/Shutterstock, 19 (child); ChristianChan/Shutterstock, 19 (equations); Ariel Skelley/Getty, 20-21; valdis torms/Shutterstock, 23.

Printed in the United States of America at Corporate Graphics in North Mankato, Minnesota.

TABLE OF CONTENTS

$$E = mc^2$$

CHAPTER 1

PHYSICS EXPERTS

Do you like roller coasters?
Guess who designed them.
A physicist!

Maglev trains have no wheels. But they do have **magnets**. These allow them to float above the tracks. Who figured this out? Physicists.

They are experts. Of what? **Physics**. This includes **forces**. **Motion**. **Energy**. It is also fluids, light, and magnets.

They study the atom, too. And the natural world. They use math to describe it.

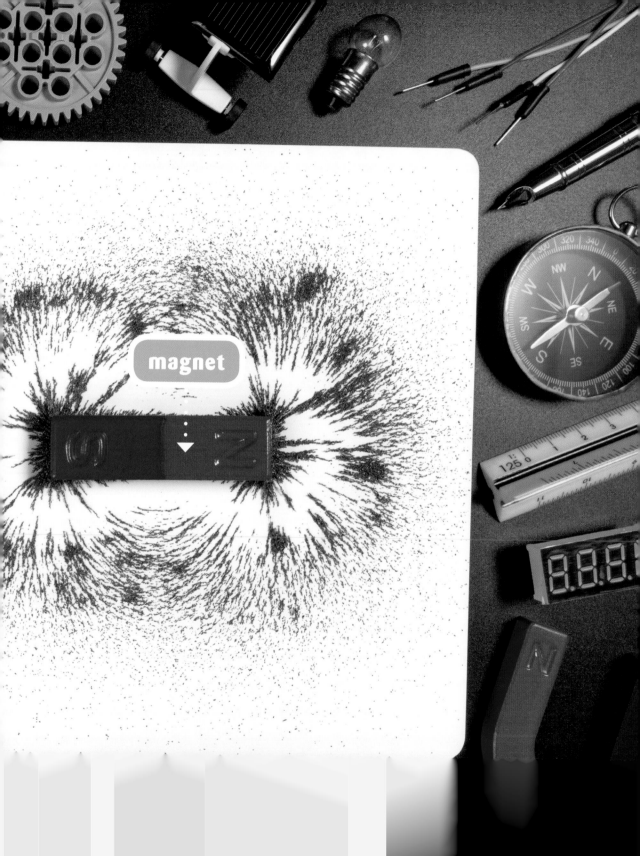

CHAPTER 2

MANY JOBS

Physicists solve problems. They use **logic**. And reasoning. They analyze **data**. These strengths help them do many types of jobs.

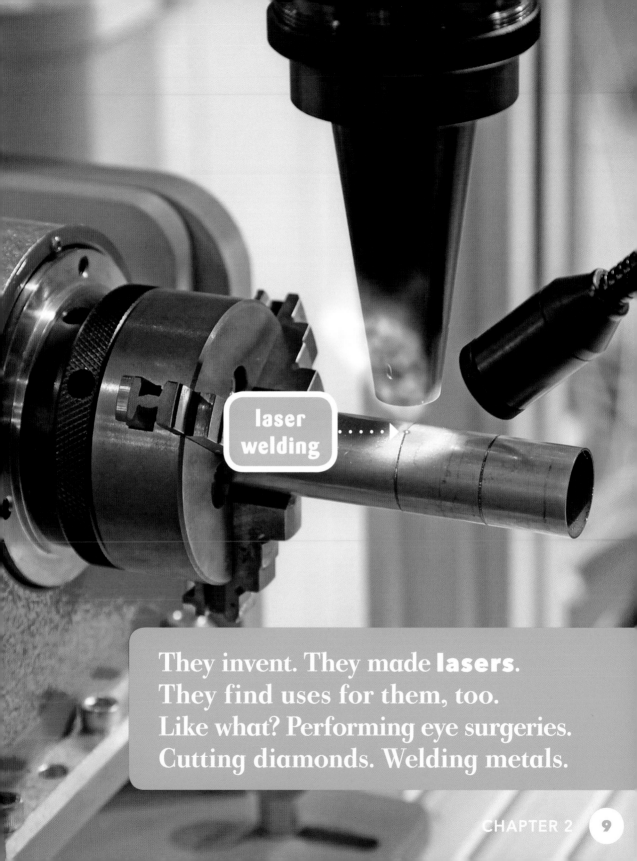

laser
welding

They invent. They made **lasers**.
They find uses for them, too.
Like what? Performing eye surgeries.
Cutting diamonds. Welding metals.

Some work with the space program. They might plan a launch. A rocket must escape Earth's **gravity**. They figure out what **velocity** it needs. How? They use data from **satellites**.

Some work on space telescopes. They study the mysteries of space.

TAKE A LOOK!

Physicists help launch rockets! They look at the different forces acting on the rocket. Some forces pull it down. Which ones? Weight and **drag**. **Thrust** pushes it up. **Lift** pushes it sideways from the direction of the thrust.

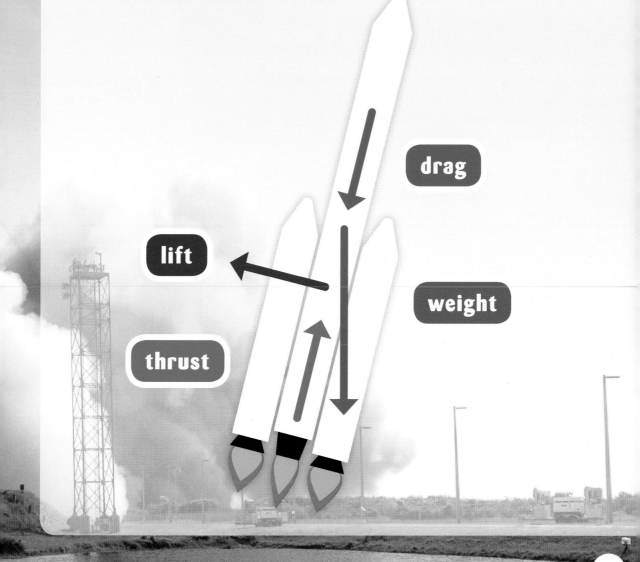

drag

lift

weight

thrust

Some work in hospitals. Doctors use **radiation**. It can treat cancer. Physicists help them. They find out how much to use.

Others help with X-rays. They write safety rules for X-ray machines. They teach people how to use them.

DID YOU KNOW?

We use X-ray machines to see into the human body. What can they see? Broken bones. Even cancer.

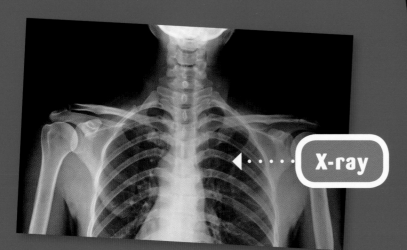

X-ray

X-ray
machine

Some work in labs. They conduct research. Experiment. Invent. They help improve wind turbines. And solar panels. Some even work with robots! They program them. To do what? Find harmful chemicals.

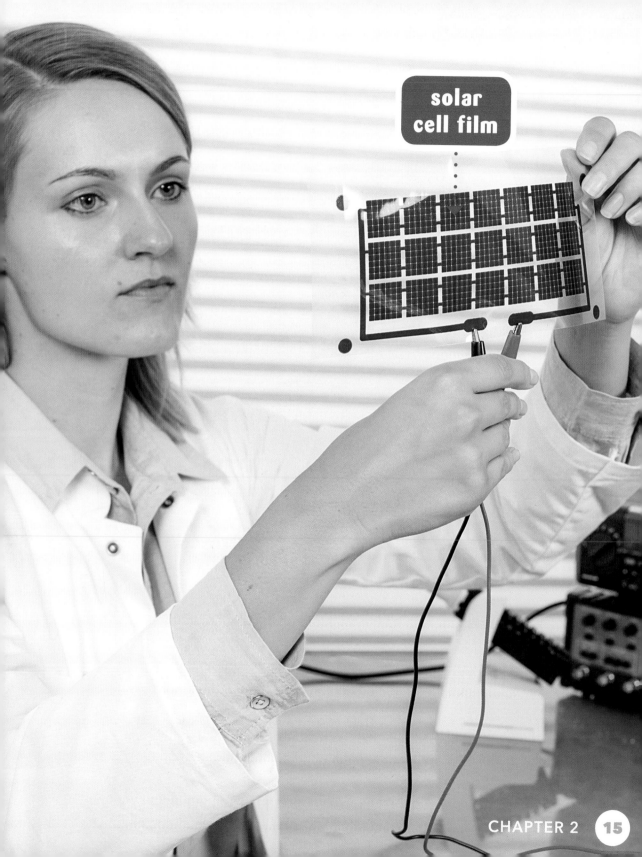

solar
cell film

SELF DRIVING
MODE

65

self-driving
car

They use science and math skills. Some write **software**. It could control a space telescope. Send and receive signals from a cell phone tower. Or guide self-driving cars.

DID YOU KNOW?

Physics is all around us! It is even in video games. Video game coders use physics to make the **graphics** realistic.

CHAPTER 3

BECOMING A PHYSICIST

To be a physicist you'll need to do many **calculations**. Do you know how to use computers?

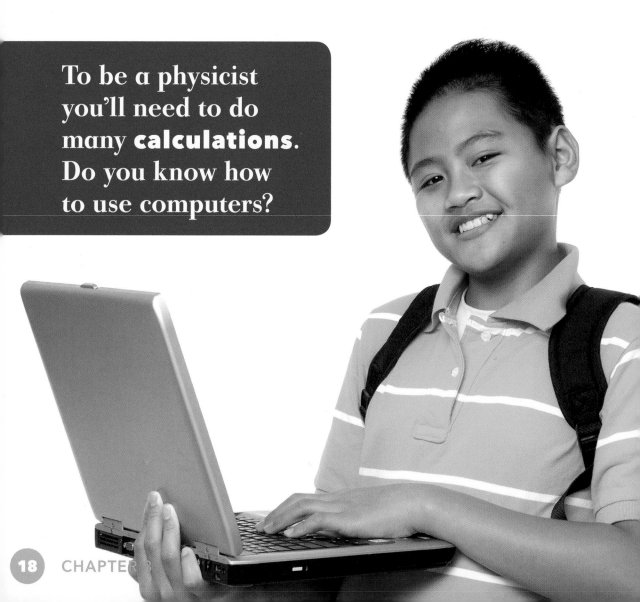

You'll need to go to college. You may need many degrees. But you don't have be a genius. Study math and science.

Do you like to experiment? Would you like to make a scientific discovery? You could change the future! You could be a physicist!

DID YOU KNOW?

To work as a physicist, you need STEM skills. What does STEM stand for? Science. Technology. Engineering. Math. STEM careers are in demand. They pay well, too.

ACTIVITIES & TOOLS

ELECTROMAGNET ACTIVITY

Electricity and magnets are both areas of physics. Have an adult help you use electricity to create a magnet.

What You Need:
- 3-inch iron, steel, or zinc nail (not aluminum)
- 2 feet of thin coated copper wire
- size D battery
- electrical tape
- small items to test magnetism, such as paper clips, a thin strip of aluminum foil, thumbtacks, a washer, a screw, a piece of yarn, or a rubber band
- paper and pencil

❶ Wrap the copper wire tightly around the nail several times. Do not overlap the wire loops. Leave about 8 to 10 inches of extra wire off each end of the nail.

❷ Peel about an inch of coating off each end of the copper wire.

❸ Place one end of the copper wire on the top battery post. Tape it in place.

❹ Place the other end of the copper wire on the bottom of the battery. Tape it in place. Be careful! The wire can get hot.

❺ Touch each small item to the nail to see if each is magnetic. Record the results on your paper.

❻ Disconnect the wire from the battery as soon as your tests are complete. The connection will quickly drain the battery.

GLOSSARY

calculations: Amounts or numbers figured out by using mathematics.

data: Facts about something.

drag: A force that goes against the motion of an object.

energy: The ability to do work.

forces: Actions that produce, stop, or change the shape or movement of an object.

graphics: Pictures displayed on a computer screen.

gravity: The force that pulls objects to Earth.

lasers: Machines that produce a narrow beam of light that can be used for many things.

lift: The force that goes against weight and gravity in an aircraft or spacecraft, helping it fly.

logic: Good or valid reasoning.

magnets: Pieces of metal that attract iron or steel. Magnets have two ends, which are called the north and south poles.

motion: The act of moving.

physics: The science that deals with matter and energy and their actions upon each other.

radiation: The emission or transmission of energy in the form of waves or particles.

satellites: Machines that are sent into space to circle Earth, the moon, the sun, or another planet.

software: The programs that run on a computer and accomplish certain functions.

thrust: The force that moves aircraft or spacecraft forward.

velocity: Speed.

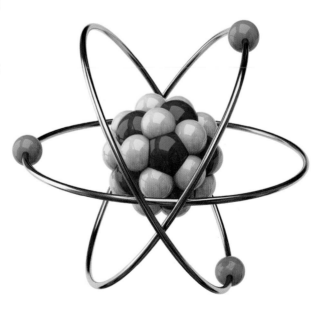

INDEX

TO LEARN MORE

Finding more information is as easy as 1, 2, 3.

1 Go to www.factsurfer.com

2 Enter "physicist" into the search box.

3 Click the "Surf" button to see a list of websites.

FACT SURFER